Collins

easy le

Fractions

quick quizzes

Ages 5–7

$\frac{1}{3}$ $\frac{1}{2}$? $\frac{1}{3}$ $\frac{1}{4}$

Angela Smith

Half of a shape

Colour the shape that shows two halves.

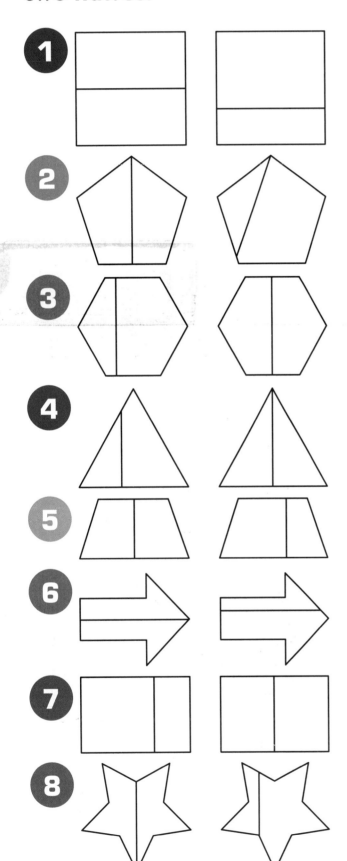

Colour your score

Halving shapes

Draw a line to divide each shape in half.

If the two parts are not equal, they are not halves.

1

2

3

4

5

6

7

8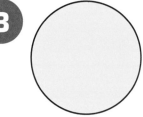

9

10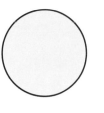

10
9
8
7
6
5
4
3
2
1

Colour your score

Half of a set

How many is $\frac{1}{2}$?

Draw a ring around $\frac{1}{2}$ the objects and write your answer.

1

2

3

4

5

6

7

8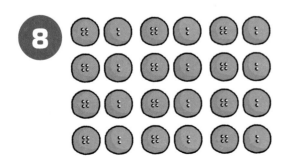

Colour your score

8
7
6
5
4
3
2
1

Halving sets

Colour $\frac{1}{2}$ of the objects.

Write the number you have coloured.

The same number of objects should be coloured and not coloured.

1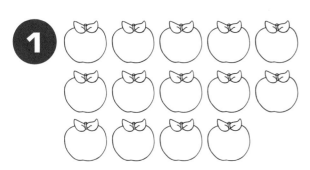

2

3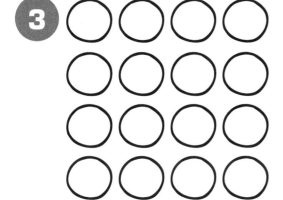

4

5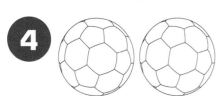

6

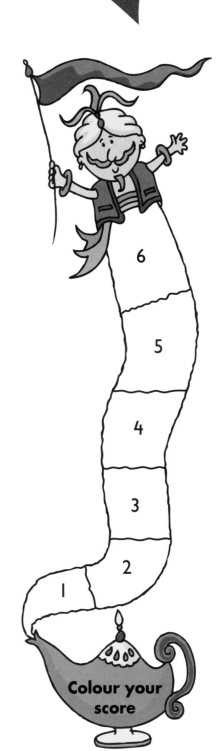

Colour your score

Half each

Share the spots equally between the ladybird's two wings.

1 6 spots

5 2 spots

2 14 spots

6 16 spots

3 10 spots

7 4 spots

4 8 spots

8 12 spots

Colour your score

Sharing between two

Draw rings around the animals to share them equally between the homes.

Sharing between two is halving.

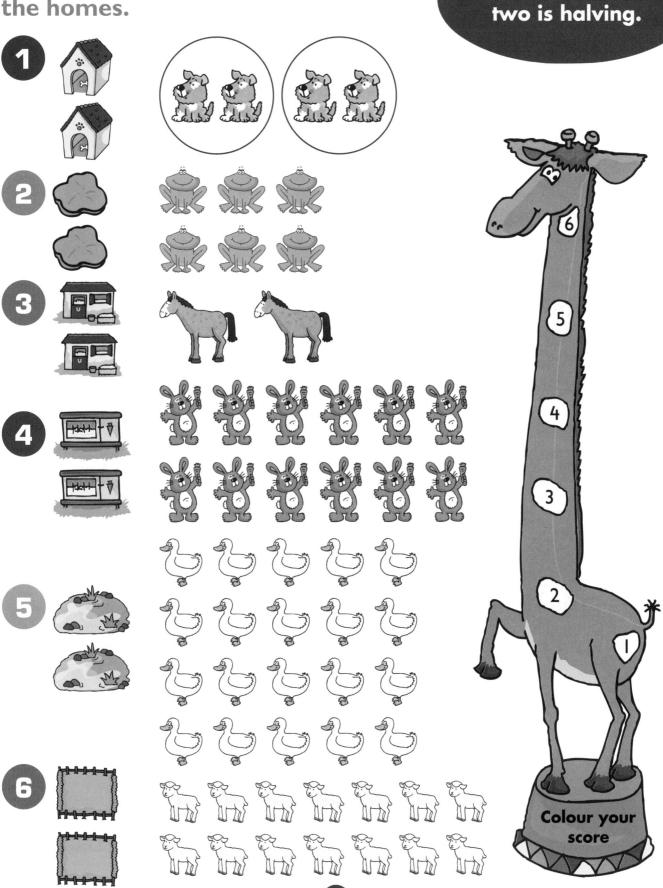

Colour your score

7

Half of a number

Find $\frac{1}{2}$ of each number.

1 $\frac{1}{2}$ of 10 ➡️ ☐

2 $\frac{1}{2}$ of 4 ➡️ ☐

3 $\frac{1}{2}$ of 20 ➡️ ☐

4 $\frac{1}{2}$ of 12 ➡️ ☐

5 $\frac{1}{2}$ of 16 ➡️ ☐

6 $\frac{1}{2}$ of 2 ➡️ ☐

7 $\frac{1}{2}$ of 18 ➡️ ☐

8 $\frac{1}{2}$ of 6 ➡️ ☐

9 $\frac{1}{2}$ of 24 ➡️ ☐

10 $\frac{1}{2}$ of 8 ➡️ ☐

11 $\frac{1}{2}$ of 14 ➡️ ☐

12 $\frac{1}{2}$ of 22 ➡️ ☐

To find half of a number, divide by two.

Colour your score

Half measures

Find $\frac{1}{2}$ of each amount.

1 $\frac{1}{2}$ of 8 cm ➡ ☐ cm

2 $\frac{1}{2}$ of 12 p ➡ ☐ p

3 $\frac{1}{2}$ of 16 g ➡ ☐ g

4 $\frac{1}{2}$ of £10 ➡ £☐

5 $\frac{1}{2}$ of 4 m ➡ ☐ m

6 $\frac{1}{2}$ of £6 ➡ £☐

7 $\frac{1}{2}$ of 18 kg ➡ ☐ kg

8 $\frac{1}{2}$ of 2 cm ➡ ☐ cm

9 $\frac{1}{2}$ of 20 p ➡ ☐ p

10 $\frac{1}{2}$ of 12 g ➡ ☐ g

11 $\frac{1}{2}$ of 10 m ➡ ☐ m

12 $\frac{1}{2}$ of £16 ➡ £☐

13 $\frac{1}{2}$ of 6 kg ➡ ☐ kg

14 $\frac{1}{2}$ of 4 p ➡ ☐ p

15 $\frac{1}{2}$ of 14 cm ➡ ☐ cm

Treat measures the same as any other numbers.

Colour your score

9

Quarters

Colour one quarter of each shape.
Write the number of parts coloured.

1

6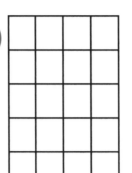

2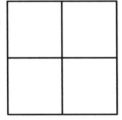

7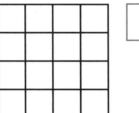

3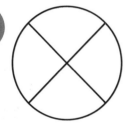

8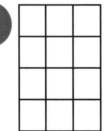

4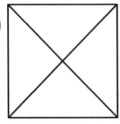

9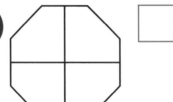

5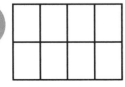

10

To quarter, you halve the number of parts in the shape and then halve again.

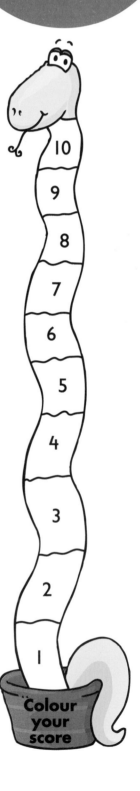

10
9
8
7
6
5
4
3
2
1

Colour your score

Quarter of a shape

Colour the shape that shows four quarters.

1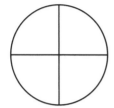

2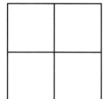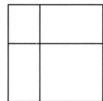

3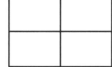

4

5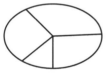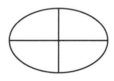

6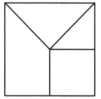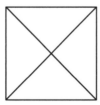

7

8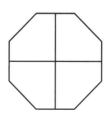

A shape divided into quarters has four equal parts.

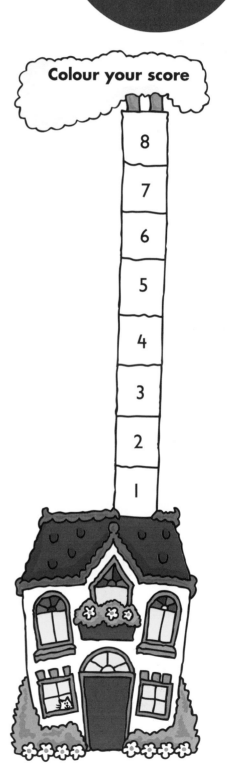

Colour your score

8
7
6
5
4
3
2
1

Half and half again

Draw a line to divide each shape in half. Then divide it in half again to make quarters.

Find different ways to divide each shape into quarters.

Try drawing diagonal lines on one of the shapes in each pair.

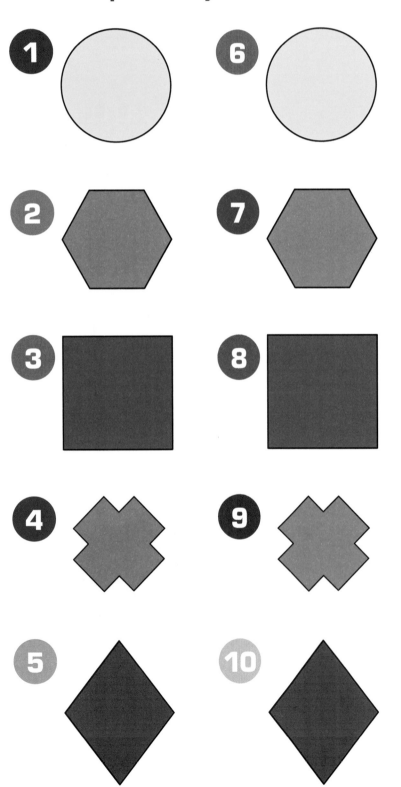

Colour your score

Quartering shapes

Draw two lines to divide each
shape into quarters.

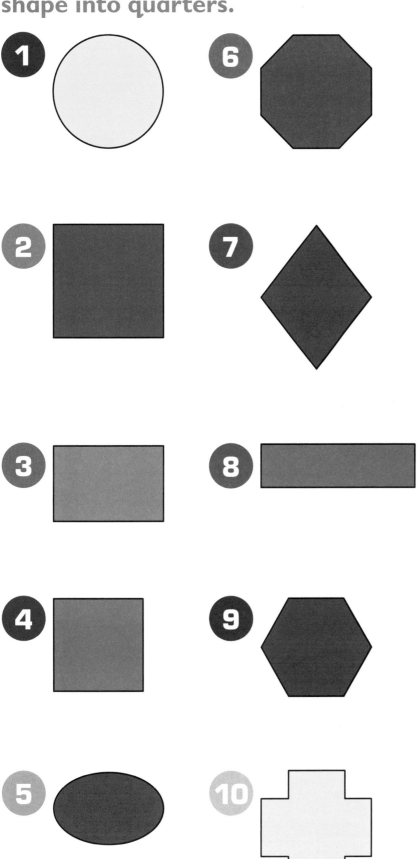

1

2

3

4

5

6

7

8

9

10

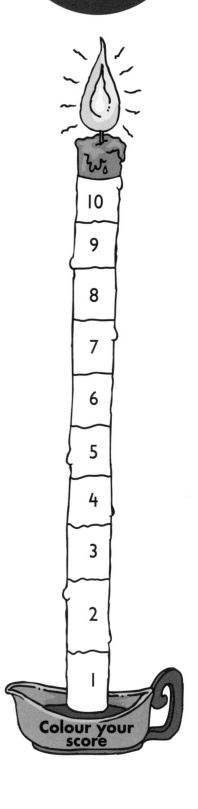

10

9

8

7

6

5

4

3

2

1

Colour your
score

Quarter of a set

How many is $\frac{1}{4}$?

Draw a circle around $\frac{1}{4}$ of the objects and write the answer.

To find $\frac{1}{4}$, divide by four.

1

2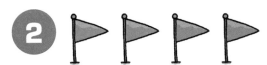

3

4

5

6

7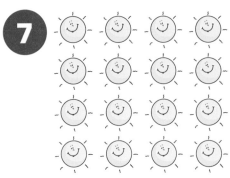

8

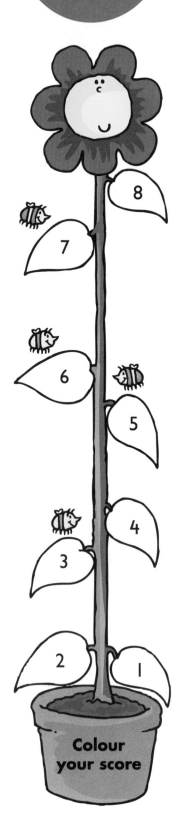

Colour your score

8
7
6
5
4
3
2
1

Finding one quarter

Colour $\frac{1}{4}$ of each set of objects.
Write the number you have coloured.

Remember to divide by four.

1

2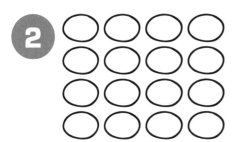

3

4

5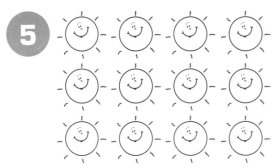

6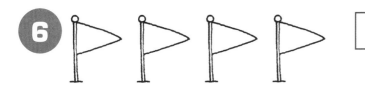

Colour your score

Sharing between four

Draw rings around the food to share it between the animals.

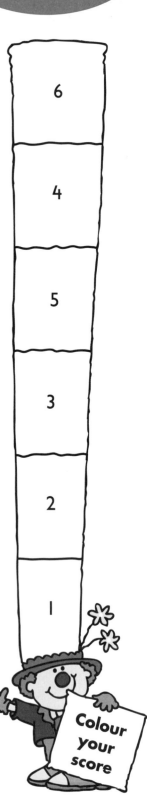

If you share between four, you are finding $\frac{1}{4}$ of a number.

1

2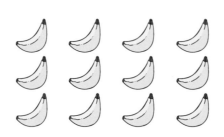

3

4

5

6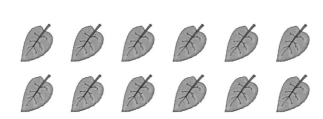

Colour your score

Equivalent fractions

Put a tick if both pictures show $\frac{1}{2}$.
Put a cross if not.

$\frac{2}{4}$ is the same as $\frac{1}{2}$.

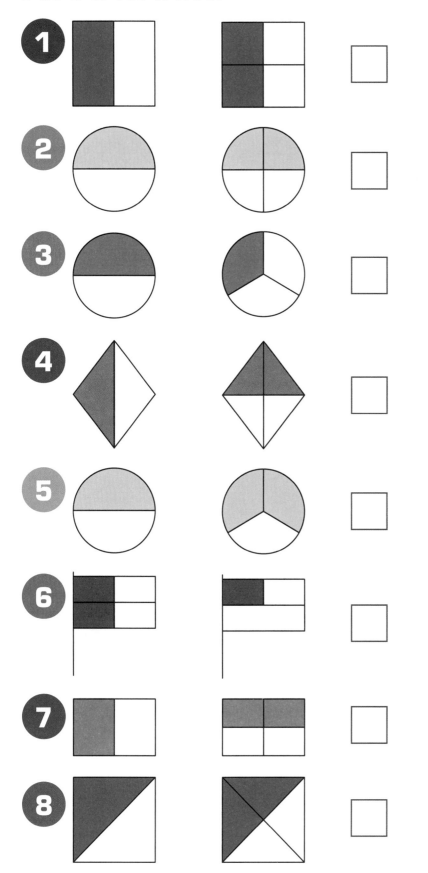

1

2

3

4

5

6

7

8

Colour your score

Quarter of a number

What is $\frac{1}{4}$ of each amount?

1 $\frac{1}{4}$ of 8 ➡️ ☐

2 $\frac{1}{4}$ of 12 ➡️ ☐

3 $\frac{1}{4}$ of 4 ➡️ ☐

4 $\frac{1}{4}$ of 16 ➡️ ☐

5 $\frac{1}{4}$ of 24 ➡️ ☐

6 $\frac{1}{4}$ of 20 ➡️ ☐

7 $12 \div 4$ ➡️ ☐

8 $4 \div 4$ ➡️ ☐

9 $8 \div 4$ ➡️ ☐

10 $16 \div 4$ ➡️ ☐

11 $24 \div 4$ ➡️ ☐

12 $20 \div 4$ ➡️ ☐

Remember, to find $\frac{1}{4}$, you divide by four.

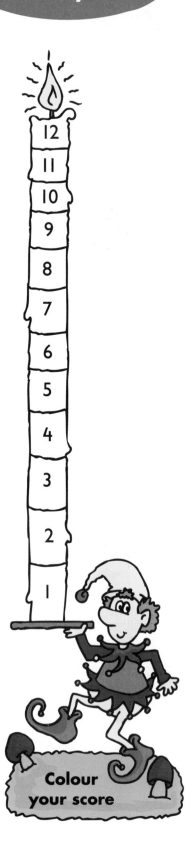

Colour your score

Quarter measures

Find $\frac{1}{4}$ of each amount.

1. $\frac{1}{4}$ of 4 cm ➡ ☐ cm

2. $\frac{1}{4}$ of 12 p ➡ ☐ p

3. $\frac{1}{4}$ of 20 g ➡ ☐ g

4. $\frac{1}{4}$ of 16 litres ➡ ☐ litres

5. $\frac{1}{4}$ of 8 m ➡ ☐ m

6. $\frac{1}{4}$ of £4 ➡ £ ☐

7. $\frac{1}{4}$ of 12 kg ➡ ☐ kg

8. $\frac{1}{4}$ of 8 litres ➡ ☐ litres

9. $\frac{1}{4}$ of 20 cm ➡ ☐ cm

10. $\frac{1}{4}$ of 16 g ➡ ☐ g

11. $\frac{1}{4}$ of 4 m ➡ ☐ m

12. $\frac{1}{4}$ of £20 ➡ £ ☐

13. $\frac{1}{4}$ of 8 kg ➡ ☐ kg

14. $\frac{1}{4}$ of 16 cm ➡ ☐ cm

15. $\frac{1}{4}$ of 8 p ➡ ☐ p

Colour your score

One third

Colour one third of each shape. How many pieces have you coloured?

One third is one of three equal parts.

1 ⬜

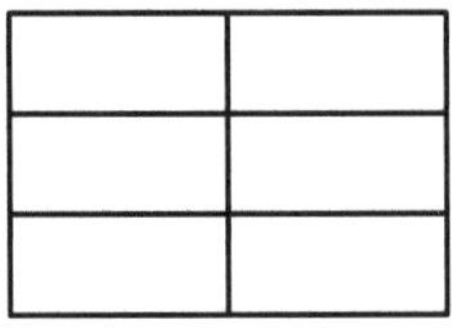

6 ⬜

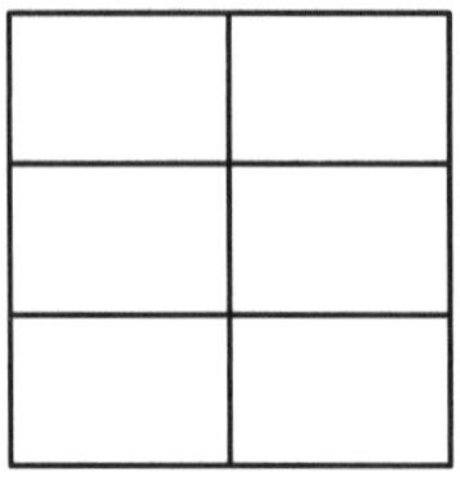

2 ⬜

7 ⬜

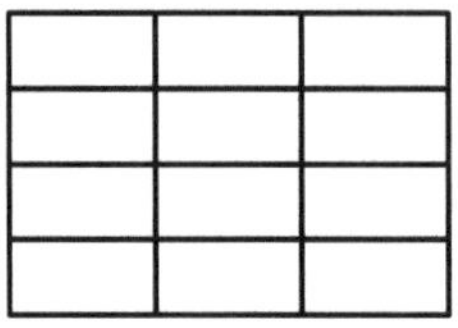

3 ⬜

8 ⬜

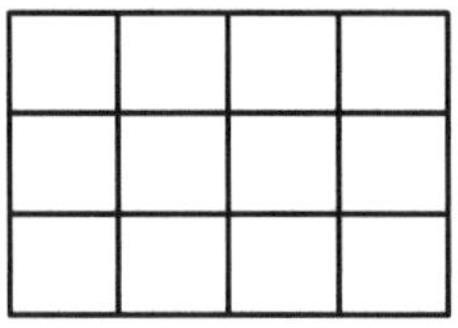

4 ⬜

9 ⬜

5 ⬜

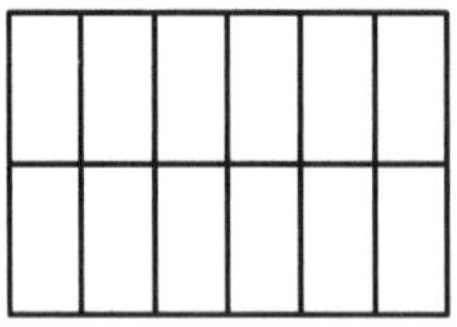

10 ⬜

10
9
8
7
6
5
4
3
2
1

Colour your score

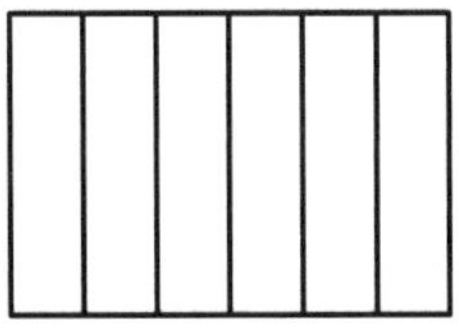

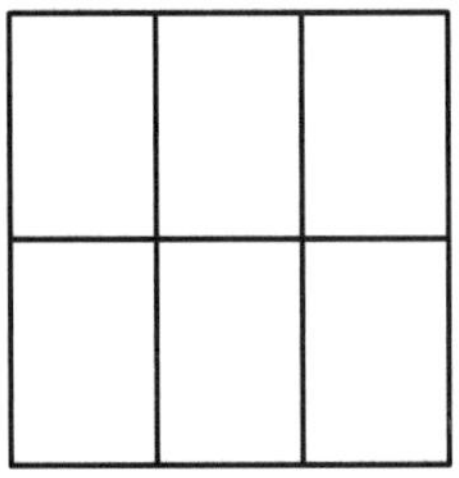

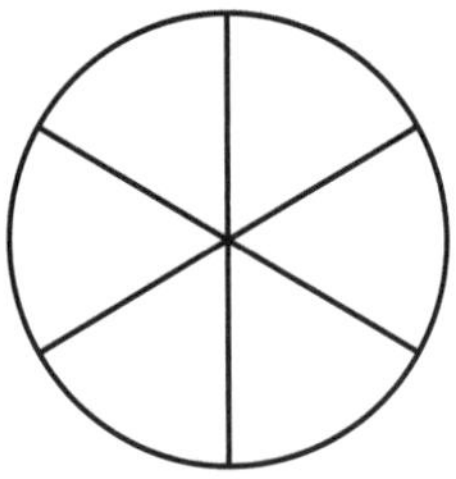

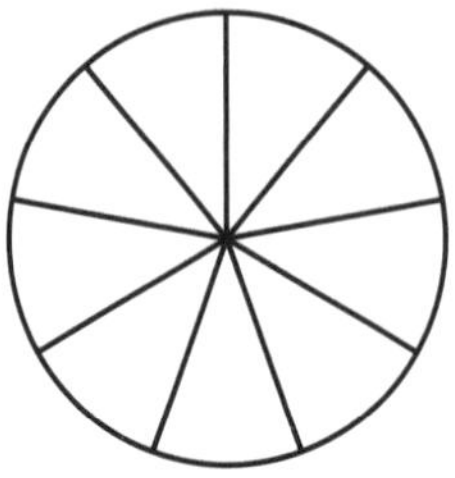

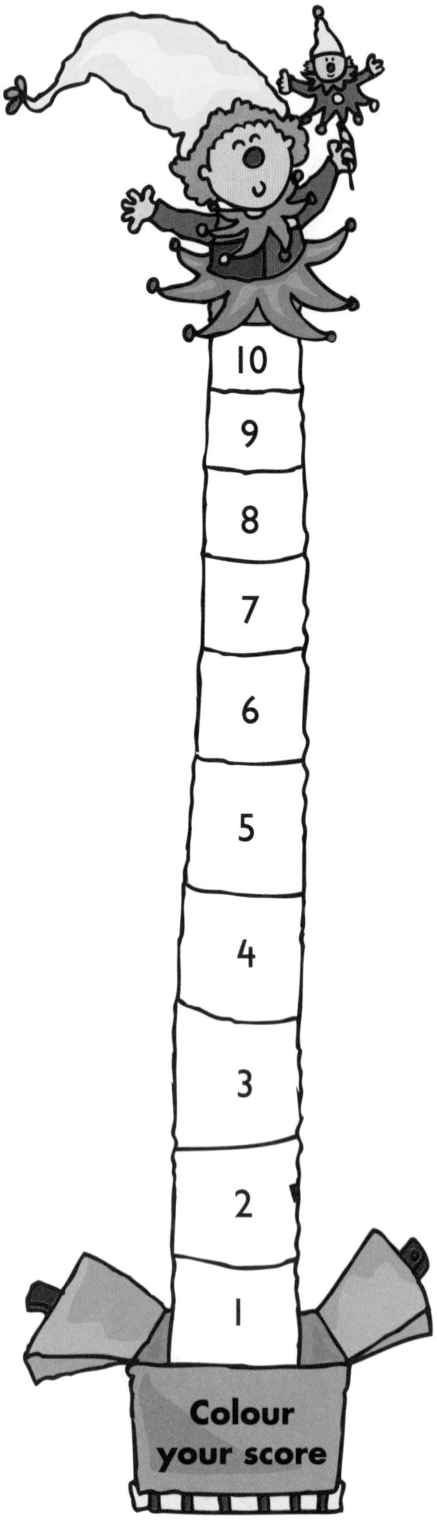

One third of a set

How many is $\frac{1}{3}$?

Draw a circle around $\frac{1}{3}$ of the objects and write the answer.

To find $\frac{1}{3}$, divide the total number by three.

1   ☐

2   ☐

3   ☐

4   ☐

5   ☐

6  ☐

7     ☐

8    ☐

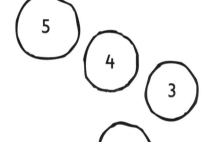

Colour your score

21

Finding one third

Draw rings around the objects to share them between the containers.

If you share between three, each share is $\frac{1}{3}$ of the number.

1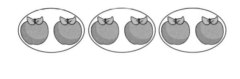

2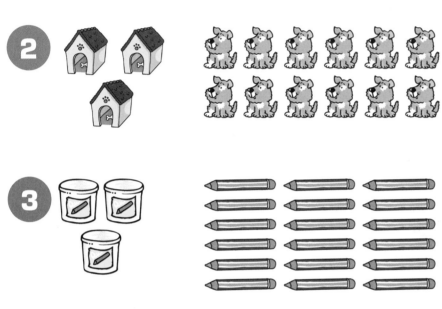

3

4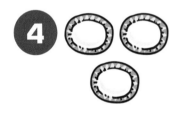

5

6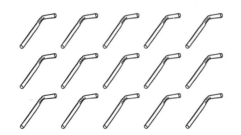

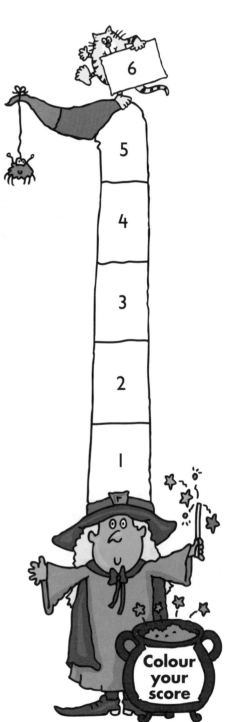

6

5

4

3

2

1

Colour your score

22

One third of a number

What is $\frac{1}{3}$ of each amount?

1 $\frac{1}{3}$ of 6 ➡️ ☐

2 $\frac{1}{3}$ of 3 ➡️ ☐

3 $\frac{1}{3}$ of 12 ➡️ ☐

4 $\frac{1}{3}$ of 9 ➡️ ☐

5 $\frac{1}{3}$ of 15 ➡️ ☐

6 $\frac{1}{3}$ of 21 ➡️ ☐

7 $3 \div 3$ ➡️ ☐

8 $12 \div 3$ ➡️ ☐

9 $6 \div 3$ ➡️ ☐

10 $9 \div 3$ ➡️ ☐

11 $15 \div 3$ ➡️ ☐

12 $21 \div 3$ ➡️ ☐

To find a fraction of an amount, you divide by the bottom number.

Colour your score

One third measures

Find $\frac{1}{3}$ of each amount.

1 $\frac{1}{3}$ of 3 cm ➡ ☐ cm

2 $\frac{1}{3}$ of 15 g ➡ ☐ g

3 $\frac{1}{3}$ of 9 p ➡ ☐ p

4 $\frac{1}{3}$ of 6 litres ➡ ☐ litres

5 $\frac{1}{3}$ of 15 m ➡ ☐ m

6 $\frac{1}{3}$ of £6 ➡ £ ☐

7 $\frac{1}{3}$ of 12 kg ➡ ☐ kg

8 $\frac{1}{3}$ of 21 cm ➡ ☐ cm

9 $\frac{1}{3}$ of 18 g ➡ ☐ g

10 $\frac{1}{3}$ of 3 p ➡ ☐ p

11 $\frac{1}{3}$ of 15 litres ➡ ☐ litres

12 $\frac{1}{3}$ of 12 m ➡ ☐ m

13 $\frac{1}{3}$ of 21 kg ➡ ☐ kg

14 $\frac{1}{3}$ of £15 ➡ £ ☐

15 $\frac{1}{3}$ of 18 cm ➡ ☐ cm

To find $\frac{1}{3}$, divide by three.

Colour your score

24

Counting in fractions

Fill in the missing fractions in each sequence.

Some of the sequences count up, others count down.

1 0, $\frac{1}{2}$, ☐, $1\frac{1}{2}$, ☐

2 $2\frac{1}{2}$, 3, ☐, 4, ☐

3 1, ☐, 2, $2\frac{1}{2}$, ☐

4 4, ☐, 3, $2\frac{1}{2}$, ☐

5 2, $1\frac{1}{2}$, ☐, $\frac{1}{2}$, ☐

6 0, $\frac{1}{4}$, $\frac{2}{4}$, ☐, ☐

7 1, $1\frac{1}{4}$, ☐, $1\frac{3}{4}$, ☐

8 2, $2\frac{1}{4}$, ☐, $2\frac{3}{4}$, ☐

9 1, $\frac{3}{4}$, ☐, $\frac{1}{4}$, ☐

10 3, $2\frac{3}{4}$, ☐, $2\frac{1}{4}$, ☐

11 0, ☐, $\frac{2}{3}$, 1, ☐

12 2, ☐, $2\frac{2}{3}$, ☐, $3\frac{1}{3}$

13 1, ☐, $1\frac{2}{3}$, 2, ☐

14 3, $2\frac{2}{3}$, ☐, 2, ☐

15 ☐, 1, $\frac{2}{3}$, ☐, 0

Colour your score

25

Mixed fractions

Write the fraction of each number.

Remember, divide by the bottom number of the fraction.

1 $\frac{1}{4}$ of 12 ➡ ☐

2 $\frac{1}{2}$ of 8 ➡ ☐

3 $\frac{1}{3}$ of 12 ➡ ☐

4 $\frac{1}{4}$ of 8 ➡ ☐

5 $\frac{1}{2}$ of 6 ➡ ☐

6 $\frac{1}{3}$ of 9 ➡ ☐

7 $\frac{1}{2}$ of 20 ➡ ☐

8 $\frac{1}{2}$ of 4 ➡ ☐

9 $\frac{1}{3}$ of 15 ➡ ☐

10 $\frac{1}{4}$ of 16 ➡ ☐

11 $\frac{1}{4}$ of 20 ➡ ☐

12 $\frac{1}{2}$ of 12 ➡ ☐

13 $\frac{1}{3}$ of 30 ➡ ☐

14 $\frac{1}{4}$ of 24 ➡ ☐

15 $\frac{1}{3}$ of 6 ➡ ☐

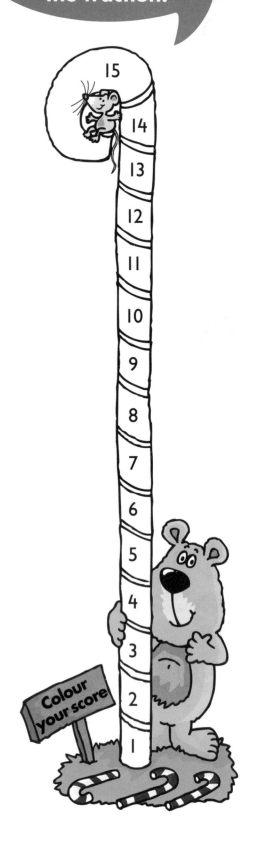

Colour your score

15 14 13 12 11 10 9 8 7 6 5 4 3 2 1

More mixed fractions

Write the fraction of each number.

1 $\frac{1}{3}$ of 9 ➡️ ☐

2 $\frac{1}{2}$ of 24 ➡️ ☐

3 $\frac{1}{4}$ of 20 ➡️ ☐

4 $\frac{1}{3}$ of 21 ➡️ ☐

5 $\frac{1}{2}$ of 16 ➡️ ☐

6 $\frac{1}{4}$ of 8 ➡️ ☐

7 $\frac{1}{3}$ of 3 ➡️ ☐

8 $\frac{1}{2}$ of 10 ➡️ ☐

9 $\frac{1}{4}$ of 16 ➡️ ☐

10 $\frac{1}{2}$ of 12 ➡️ ☐

11 $\frac{1}{3}$ of 15 ➡️ ☐

12 $\frac{1}{4}$ of 24 ➡️ ☐

13 $\frac{1}{2}$ of 20 ➡️ ☐

14 $\frac{1}{3}$ of 12 ➡️ ☐

15 $\frac{1}{2}$ of 18 ➡️ ☐

Remember, the bottom number of the fraction tells you what to divide by.

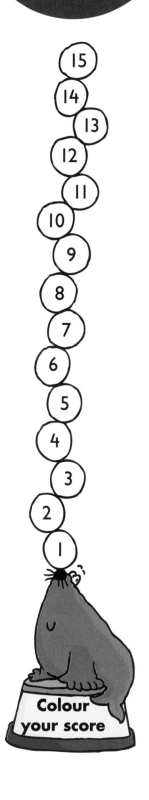

Colour your score

Three quarters of a shape

Colour $\frac{3}{4}$ of each shape.
Write down how many pieces you have coloured.

Count how many pieces make $\frac{1}{4}$.
Then times it by three to make $\frac{3}{4}$.

1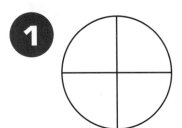

2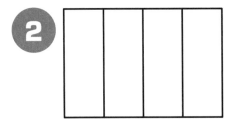

3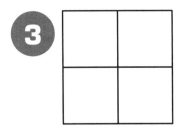

4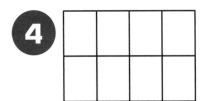

5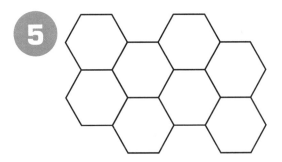

6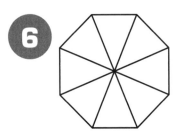

Colour your score

Three quarters of a set

How many is $\frac{3}{4}$?

Circle $\frac{3}{4}$ of the objects and write your answer.

Find $\frac{1}{4}$. Then work out how many are in $\frac{3}{4}$.

1

2

3

4

5

6

7

8

Colour your score

Finding three quarters

How many is $\frac{3}{4}$?

Colour $\frac{3}{4}$ of the objects and write your answer.

Divide by four to find $\frac{1}{4}$. Then multiply by three to find $\frac{3}{4}$.

1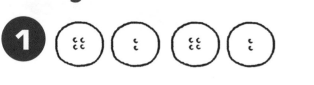

2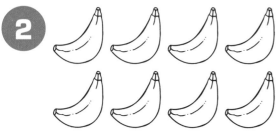

3

4

5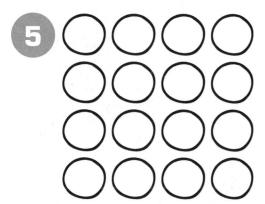

6

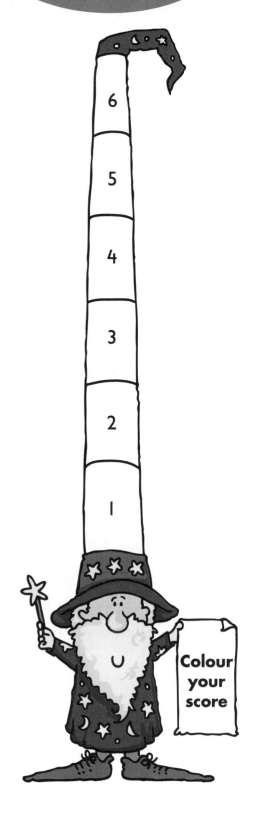

Colour your score

30

Fraction problems

Solve these real life fraction problems.

1 There were 12 apples on a tree.
Lucy picked $\frac{1}{2}$ of them.
How many were left?

2 There are 8 people on a bus.
$\frac{1}{4}$ of them are children.
How many children are on
the bus?

3 There are 15 sweets in a box.
Georgia eats $\frac{1}{3}$ of them.
How many sweets does
she eat?

4 There are 20 children in Class 2.
$\frac{1}{2}$ of them are boys.
How many boys are in
the class?

5 There are 9 children in a sports group.
$\frac{1}{3}$ of them play football.
How many children play
football?

6 There are 12 biscuits in a tin.
$\frac{1}{4}$ get eaten.
How many biscuits are eaten?

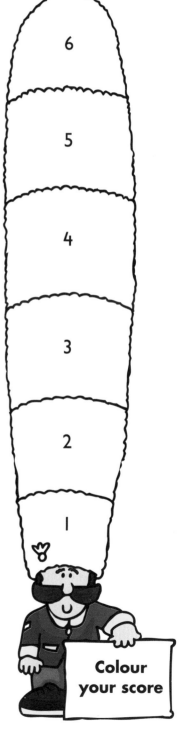

Read the questions carefully. Use the skills you have learnt so far.

6
5
4
3
2
1

Colour your score

31

Answers

Half of a shape

1.
2.
3.
4.
5.
6.
7.
8.

Halving shapes

All shapes must be divided exactly in half. The pictures below give just one way of doing this.

1.
2.
3.
4.
5.
6.
7.
8.
9.
10.

Half of a set

1. 3
2. 5
3. 4
4. 6
5. 1
6. 7
7. 8
8. 12

Halving sets

1. 7
2. 2
3. 8
4. 1
5. 6
6. 3

Half each

The following number of spots should be drawn on each wing:

1. 3
2. 7
3. 5
4. 4
5. 1
6. 8
7. 2
8. 6

Sharing between two

The following number of animals should be in each ringed group:

1. 2
2. 3
3. 1
4. 6
5. 10
6. 7

Half of a number

1. 5
2. 2
3. 10
4. 6
5. 8
6. 1
7. 9
8. 3
9. 12
10. 4
11. 7
12. 11

Half measures

1. 4 cm
2. 6 p
3. 8 g
4. £5
5. 2 m
6. £3
7. 9 kg
8. 1 cm
9. 10 p
10. 6 g
11. 5 m
12. £8
13. 3 kg
14. 2 p
15. 7 cm

Quarters

1. 1
2. 1
3. 1
4. 1
5. 2
6. 5
7. 4
8. 3
9. 1
10. 1

Quarter of a shape

1.
2.
3.
4.
5.
6.
7.
8.

Half and half again

All shapes must be divided exactly into quarters. The pictures below are examples of how this may be done.

1.
2.
3.
4.
5.
6.
7.
8.
9.
10.

Quartering shapes

All shapes must be divided exactly into quarters. The pictures below are examples of how this may be done.

1.
2.
3.
4.
5.
6.
7.
8.
9.
10.

Quarter of a set

1. 2
2. 1
3. 5
4. 4
5. 6
6. 1
7. 4
8. 3

Finding one quarter

1. 3
2. 4
3. 2
4. 5
5. 3
6. 1

Sharing between four

The following number of items should be in each ringed group:

1. 2
2. 3
3. 1
4. 2
5. 1
6. 3

Equivalent fractions

1. ✓
2. ✓
3. ✗
4. ✓
5. ✗
6. ✗
7. ✓
8. ✓

Quarter of a number

1. 2
2. 3
3. 1
4. 4
5. 6
6. 5
7. 3
8. 1
9. 2
10. 4
11. 6
12. 5

Quarter measures

1. 1 cm
2. 3 p
3. 5 g
4. 4 litres